Original title:
Wristbands of the Soul

Copyright © 2025 Creative Arts Management OÜ
All rights reserved.

Author: Arabella Whitmore
ISBN HARDBACK: 978-1-80586-148-5
ISBN PAPERBACK: 978-1-80586-620-6

Adrift in a Sea of Sentiment

I floated on a wave of feels,
Like rubber ducks on spinning wheels.
With every splash, a giggle grew,
My heart's a boat that's lost its crew.

Emotions whirl like whirlpool brine,
I can't recall if they're yours or mine.
A tugboat's pull, a gentle jest,
Yet still I grin and feel quite blessed.

The Dance of Ties and Tribes

We shuffle feet in mismatched shoes,
Each twirl a step, no room for blues.
A conga line of quirks, oh my!
Where everyone's a silly spy.

Their laughter's bait, it hooks my soul,
With playful pranks, we share the goal.
In this funny jig, together we sway,
Binding hearts with joy each day.

From Heartstrings to Ether

My heartstrings hum a silly tune,
A melody beneath the moon.
I float like clouds, so soft and free,
In the breeze of sweet absurdity.

With giddy jests and vibrant beams,
We thread our hopes like patchwork dreams.
In laughter's light, we dance and play,
The thread of life won't fray away.

Silhouettes and Bonds of Being

We cast our shadows on the ground,
In shapes and forms that twist around.
Like playful puppets, we take flight,
With every giggle, day turns bright.

Our silhouettes in jest combine,
A tapestry, so sweetly fine.
With each embrace, a funny quirk,
In life's strange dance, we find our work.

Whispered Dreams of Togetherness

In a world of colors bright,
We find our laughs take flight.
With silly hats and dance so free,
We juggle friendship, you and me.

Calling out, we play our games,
Wearing silly, mismatched names.
With ice cream on our noses strong,
We skip along, just singing songs.

The sun may shine, or it may pout,
But together, there's no doubt.
We trip and tumble, grace on pause,
Yet friendship's always got our cause.

In moments shared, we stitch our tales,
With giggles soaring, like the sails.
So here's to weaving joy so grand,
With laughter tied, we make our stand.

Echoes of the Heart's Ties

Amidst the chaos, giggles sound,
With every fumble, love is found.
We dance like penguins, oh so fine,
With hearts that giggle, yours and mine.

Oh, mischief wrapped in silly charm,
We spin and twirl without alarm.
Like spaghetti noodles in a heap,
Our bond is strong, not one to sweep.

In whispers shared beneath the moon,
We stir the night with a funny tune.
With playful jabs and friendly jests,
Our laughter surely beats the rest.

So raise your glass to quirky dreams,
A toast to life beyond the seams.
With every chuckle, hugs will flow,
In echoes bright, our spirits glow.

Colors of Unity and Faith

In a world so bright and loud,
We wear our hues, and stand so proud.
The red brings laughter, blue knows calm,
Together we form a vibrant psalm.

Mix a yellow with a greenish light,
You never know, it might feel right.
With every shade, we dance and sway,
Creating memories that forever play.

The Invisible Bind

We're all connected, can't you see?
Tangled thoughts in a cup of tea.
Invisible strings that pull us near,
Especially when there's cake and cheer!

So when the world feels far apart,
Just grab a friend and share your heart.
With laughter echoing in the air,
We're bound together beyond compare.

Mosaic of Shared Souls

A jigsaw puzzle with missing parts,
We fit together with glowing hearts.
Each quirky piece has its own tale,
Creating a mosaic that will not fail.

With mismatched socks and crazy hats,
Laughter echoes as we share our chats.
One silly dance, and off we go,
In this tapestry, we steal the show.

Silken Ties of Belonging

Like spaghetti strands on a plate,
We twist and twirl, it's never late.
A web of giggles, a net of glee,
Binding us close, just you and me.

So let's wrap up in our tales of fun,
With silly jokes and races to run.
These ties are soft, not tight or stiff,
Bringing us joy, that's the real gift.

The Heart's Kaleidoscope

In the dance of colors bright,
Our hearts twirl, a wondrous sight.
Laughter echoes, joy takes flight,
Like socks that vanish in the night.

Patterns shift, collide, and swirl,
As life's confetti starts to twirl.
We wear our quirks, each laugh, a pearl,
With mismatched shoes, we spin and whirl.

Unity Encounters of the Spirit

Gathered here, we're quite a crew,
With silly hats and crazy shoes.
Every quirk, we proudly rue,
While sharing snacks and nose-pointed views.

A dance-off with the kitchen broom,
We laugh till we can't breathe, it's boom!
Who knew the kitchen could be a room,
Where spirits shine and tensions zoom?

Weaving Together Our Stories

With threads of laughter, tales unfold,
Stitching moments, stories bold.
In every loop, a secret told,
As mismatched socks become pure gold.

We weave the nuts, the bolts, the glue,
A patchwork quilt of me and you.
Each tale a color, vibrant hue,
In the madness, there's love too.

Fabric of Connection's Embrace

In the fabric of fun, we mend,
Stitching smiles 'round every bend.
With flour on noses, we extend,
A tapestry where laughter transcends.

The threads may fray, but that's okay,
In every prank, we find our play.
Tangled tales lead us astray,
Yet here we stand, come what may.

Memories Knotted Together

In the drawer, they pile up tight,
Colors clash in a comical sight.
Each twist tells a tale so absurd,
Who knew a yellow could be so blurred?

Grandma's gift, with a goofy grin,
A reminder of both loss and win.
Wrapped around my wrist, oh so neat,
Makes me feel both silly and sweet.

Heartfelt Knots in Time

Tangled up with laughter and cheer,
Every loop whispers, "You were here!"
Some are vibrant, some have gone gray,
A parade of moments on display.

Friendship bands from the second grade,
All the secrets we bravely made.
Though they fray as we grow old,
Each knot's a story waiting to be told.

Adornments of Forgotten Dreams

A jumbled mess, these threads align,
Of plans we hatched on bubblegum time.
Like socks in the dryer, where'd they run?
Our dreams have had their share of fun!

Each circle tells of a whim and wish,
Like wishing on a star-shaped fish.
Some days they sparkle, some days they thud,
But they're tangled in joy, not in mud.

Symphonies in a Circle

Round and round, they play a song,
A melody where all of us belong.
Colors dance in a silly spree,
A rhythm that feels just like glee.

From blues to purples, don't forget red,
Each hue is a giggle, nothing to dread.
In the tangled mess, I find my tune,
A symphony spun beneath the moon.

Kinship in Kaleidoscopic Light

In a world where colors blend,
We wear our laughs like rainbow bends.
With mismatched socks and silly caps,
We dance like frogs in oversized claps.

Bouncing thoughts like ping pong balls,
In this circus, no one falls.
Jokes fly like stars in the night,
Chasing giggles, oh what a sight!

A bond so bright, it's hard to miss,
With silly snaps and goofy bliss.
Each chuckle binds us, tight and bold,
In our kaleidoscope, there's laughter untold.

So raise a toast with cups of cheer,
To all the quirks that bring us near.
In this vivid prism, love's our plight,
We shine together, a delightful sight.

Echoes Twined in Quietude.

In silent whispers, we share our quirks,
Like sneaky squirrels with snacky perks.
Our voices echo, a cheeky tune,
Under the watchful eye of the moon.

With nods that say more than mere words,
We jest like a flock of clueless birds.
Our secrets hidden in comic disguise,
Silly remarks that spark bright skies.

Together we giggle in shared delight,
Turning dull days into comic flight.
In quietude, our laughter's the thread,
Binding us tighter, like jelly and bread.

So let's make mischief, let's sow the fun,
In this tapestry where we all run.
The echoes twined, they softly say,
Life's a punchline—come out and play!

Threads of Connection

With silly hats and mismatched shoes,
We weave the tales that we all choose.
Each chuckle a stitch, each grin a thread,
In the quilt of laughter, we're brightly spread.

Our quirks entwined, a tapestry rare,
Like spaghetti noodles in tangled hair.
Knots of joy in a colorful mess,
In friendships stitched, we feel blessed.

Through tangled dreams and playful thoughts,
We tie our hearts in merry knots.
Each thread unravels a story new,
In our patchwork life, there's always room for two.

So let the laughs guide us along,
As we dance to the rhythm of our song.
In the threads of joy, we find our goal:
To celebrate the quirks that make us whole!

Echoes in the Fabric

In a fabric woven with giggles and glee,
We stitch our memories, you and me.
Each pattern reminds us of silly times,
Where laughter flows like nursery rhymes.

From patches of jokes to seams of cheer,
Our echoes dance, bringing us near.
We've tailored our tales, both funny and bright,
In this cloth of connection, it feels so right.

Oh, the antics that hide in the weave,
From playful pranks, it's hard to believe!
Each thread a whisper, each knot a laugh,
In this unique design, we're a quirky staff.

So let's toss confetti in the air,
In the echoes of fabric, we find flair.
Together we shine, absurd and bold,
In this comical world, our hearts unfold.

Unity in a Spectrum of Strands

In colors bright, we wrap our cheer,
A strip of laughter, light, sincere.
With every twist, a giggle made,
Friendship's fashion, never fade.

Wearing hues both bold and loud,
We strut our stuff, we laugh out proud.
With every strand, a silly tale,
Together, we'll never fail!

Oh, neon pink and ocean blue,
Our rainbow dreams are fresh and true.
In every knot, a chuckle's blend,
Through this fabric, joy won't end.

So let's create, and never stall,
A tapestry of laughs for all.
With every strand, a story's spun,
In this wild weave, we laugh, we run!

Resonance of the Unseen

Invisible threads, we tug and pull,
Our funny vibes, they always rule.
Though we can't see, we feel the cheer,
In silent strands, our joy is clear.

Like whispers shared 'round a campfire's glow,
A tickle here, a laugh, and whoa!
The bond we have is quite profound,
In giggles lost, we're ever found.

Jokes that echo through the air,
Each silent strand, a secret dare.
With every laugh, the world anew,
A silly dance, just me and you.

So clap your hands and stomp your feet,
In unseen ties, we find our beat.
With laughter's tune, we soon embrace,
This quirky vibe, our happy place!

Chains of Memory and Dream

In chains of giggles, memories cling,
Silly moments make our hearts sing.
Each link a laugh, each twist a smile,
Together we roam, mile by mile.

Jumping jacks and goofy cheers,
Indelible marks from yesteryears.
A chain of joy, it binds us tight,
With every blush, we dance with light.

Dreams entwined in a playful game,
Recalling stories that feel the same.
In wacky phases, we love to thrive,
These chains of fun, they keep us alive.

So here's to laughter, cheeky and bright,
Locking us in, day and night.
In chains of joy, our hearts take flight,
A memory book, our guiding light!

Knotting the Spirit's Whispers

In knots of chuckles, we bind our cheer,
Whispers of spirit, ever near.
Tangles of joy that never fray,
In every twist, we find our way.

Each little giggle, a playful dance,
Knotting our souls in a light-filled trance.
With every laugh, we soar above,
Creating bonds, wrapped in love.

So let's tie up our dreams in bliss,
A jumble of wishes we won't miss.
In playful bands, we'll forever sway,
Knotting hearts, come what may.

With colors bright, our spirits sing,
In this web of fun, sweet memories cling.
Through every knot, our laughter streams,
Together we craft our wildest dreams!

Celestial Ties of Affection

In a world where laughter spreads,
Our quirks are jewels in silly threads.
A twinkle here, a laugh that flies,
We're all just stars in grand disguise.

With wobbly dances and goofy grins,
The magic begins where the fun begins.
We hug our friends with utmost glee,
In this cosmic circus, we're all so free.

Beneath the moon, with dreams we ride,
On cotton clouds, we take a slide.
Giggles echo in the night,
As we twine our hearts in pure delight.

So let's paint our joy across the skies,
With bubblegum wishes and donut pies.
For every chuckle adds a thread,
In our celestial quilt, where silliness is spread.

Underneath the Surface: A Tapestry

There's a patchwork realm beneath our skin,
Where my cat's meows and my dog's grins spin.
We stitch with laughter, we thread with cheer,
In this wacky quilt, we hold each dear.

Oh! Look at Bob with his two left shoes,
Shuffling along like he can't refuse.
With mismatched socks and a funky tie,
He's the jester in our laughter sky.

We gather 'round the threadbare seams,
Plotting how to dance in our dreams.
With coffee spills and cupcake falls,
Every stitch tells tales; joy enthralls.

This tapestry of silly times,
Unravels with giggles, throws funny rhymes.
So gather close, let colors flow,
In our woven world, the fun must grow.

The Threads We Wear in Shadows

In the dim-lit corners, secrets play,
Where shadows dance with a silly sway.
An oversized hat and socks that squeak,
In this merry realm, we find our peak.

With hidden snacks and whispers so light,
We weave our fun in gentle night.
A wink and a nudge, a chuckle shared,
In our shadowland, no one is scared.

Each shadow's a thread, each laugh a glue,
A tapestry weird, yet proudly true.
We trip on dreams and messy hair,
In this odd parade, let's go anywhere!

As moonbeams shine on our playful plot,
With giggles and joy, we love a lot.
In our cloaked delight, we wear our pride,
These whimsical threads, our hearts can't hide.

Adorning the Invisible Self

Invisible crowns sit atop our heads,
With giggly charms and wiggly threads.
We dress our hearts in wild delight,
Each spark a joy, each laugh a light.

Floating on wishes, like balloons in air,
We twirl our fancies without a care.
On rainbows made from silly glue,
We wear our dreams, vibrant and true.

At the corner cafe, a space bizarre,
Where croissants dance under the quirky star.
With each silly order, a jest unfolds,
In this invisible world, our fun beholds.

So top off the cake with a wink and cheer,
For every moment we hold so dear.
Adorned in laughter, let's have a ball,
In this jester's realm, we'll never fall.

Enchanted Strands of Meaning

In a world where colors clash,
Ribbons dance with every splash.
Twists and turns in noisy cheer,
Giggles echo loud and clear.

We're tangled up, but that's our game,
Crafting bonds, never the same.
Each twist a laugh, each knot a grin,
In our mess, the fun begins.

Sparkly bits and fuzzy ties,
Hide our secrets and our lies.
Though we trip and sometimes fall,
These connections conquer all.

So wear your strings with style and flair,
Joking life without a care.
In this circus, we won't fade,
Crafting joy, a grand parade.

Imprints of Togetherness

From a canvas bright and bold,
Imprints spread like tales of old.
With quirks and quirks, we always shine,
Adventures shared, our hearts entwine.

Sticky notes on pandas' backs,
Running wild on laughter tracks.
With each misstep, we find our way,
Building chaos into play.

Doodles dance on coffee cups,
Life's a mix of ups and ups.
Each mishap's just a new design,
We sketch it out, it's all sublime.

Together we are quite the sight,
Fumbling joy in morning light.
Crafting memories that won't erase,
In this charm, we've found our place.

Medallions of Harmony

In laughter's echo, we unite,
Crafting joy from sheer delight.
Each clink and clatter sings a song,
In this symphony, we all belong.

We're all stars with different tunes,
Dancing 'neath the laughing moons.
Some out of sync, but who will care?
We're a band—no one is bare.

With every stumble, every fall,
We treasure it, we lose our all.
Life's a game of silly plays,
In harmony, we'll find our ways.

Our medallions gleam so bright,
Shining through each silly plight.
Together, let the jokes unfold,
In our hearts, the warmth takes hold.

Tapestry of Life's Emotions

In the fabric of our days,
Threads of laughter, woven ways.
Each color tells a silly joke,
In this tapestry, dreams evoke.

Pinching cheeks and poking sides,
We find humor where it hides.
With every thread, a memory made,
In this chaos, we won't fade.

Life is knitted, one stitch at a time,
With hiccups, laughter, and a rhyme.
Stitches slip, and seams may fray,
Yet we smile, come what may.

Together through each twist and bend,
Our tapestry will never end.
In every fiber, love's emotion,
We dance along this joyful ocean.

Threads of Collective Memory

In a world of quirky sights,
Weaving laughter, shining lights.
Every tale a silly thread,
Laughter echoes, joy widespread.

Bouncing through the silly scenes,
Memory dances, tickling dreams.
Each knot a moment, bright and bold,
Woven stories never grow old.

Laughter threadbare at the seams,
Tangled up in shared, wild schemes.
Frayed edges, jokes that always land,
Sewing memories, hand in hand.

So let's wear our nonsense proud,
In this patchwork, let's be loud.
Threads of fun and joy unite,
In our hearts, they feel just right.

Subtle Bindings of Intimacy

Oh, the bonds we make with glee,
Binding quirks, just you and me.
Giggles stitched in every seam,
A soft embrace, a cozy dream.

In secrets shared and laughter sworn,
Mix of giggles, love reborn.
Invisible ties, so tight and sweet,
Injokes echo, this rhythm's neat.

Stitches pull, where hearts collide,
In this craft, we take our stride.
Witty threads, a playful tune,
Through our laughter, we'll commune.

With silly faces, we create,
An art of love, a playful state.
Subtle bindings, hearts so fine,
In this tapestry, you'll be mine.

Ornaments of Silent Promises

Adorned with whispers, smiles abound,
We wear our secrets all around.
A wink, a grin, a playful tease,
In every gem, a joke that frees.

These trinkets hold our private glee,
In this game of you and me.
Unexpected gems we often wear,
With sparkles of joy, we make the fair.

A jester's cap, a clownish grin,
In silence, laughter seeps within.
Ornamented with quirky grace,
Life's silly dance, our happy place.

Silent promises, in jest we bind,
Together, we share this joyful mind.
With every sparkle, humor thrives,
In all these trinkets, laughter dives.

Journey's Emblems on Display

With each step, a goofy stride,
Collecting quirks, let's take a ride.
Emblems worn with pure delight,
Every adventure, a joke in sight.

From silly hats to mismatched shoes,
Each tale spins another muse.
Collect the laughs, they add up fast,
In this journey, we're born to last.

A map of giggles, off we go,
With every stop, our humor grows.
Souvenirs of laughter sewn,
In this wild ride, we'll never moan.

So let's parade our funny finds,
In bonds of humor, love entwined.
Journey's symbols, always gay,
In our hearts, they'll forever stay.

Canvases of Joy and Sorrow

In the circus of feelings, we paint our regrets,
With brushes of laughter, and palettes of pets.
Colors mix wildly, like socks in the wash,
Creating a masterpiece that's silly and posh.

With giggles and tears in a jumbled array,
We twirl through the canvas, come what may.
The sun laughs at shadows, they dance side by side,
In a gallery where every oddity's amplified.

Life's tapestry woven with clumsy delight,
Like a cat on a canvas, a comical sight.
Each stroke telling stories we twist into jokes,
A stand-up routine mixed with wild, woozy strokes.

So here's to our canvases, smudged and absurd,
Where joy and sorrow harmonize without word.
In the art of existence, let laughter unfold,
A masterpiece crafted with humor and gold.

The Interlaced Symphony

In the orchestra of chaos, we play with a grin,
Tangled in rhythms, let the laughter begin.
A kazoo plays a solo, while the trumpet's off cue,
Together we dance, it's a laugh-a-lot crew.

Strings of connection are latched in a knot,
Each note a reminder, we give it a shot.
The flute tries a pirouette, the drum takes a fall,
Creating a symphony that's joyful for all.

When melodies mingle and harmonies clash,
It's a cacophony, bursting forth with a splash.
We orchestrate giggles, compose with some flair,
Every tickle of laughter fills up the air!

So raise up your voices, let the music ignite,
In the grand interlace of wrong and of right.
A concert of fun, with each quirk and each flaw,
Together we jam, and leave the world in awe.

Echoes Beneath the Surface

In the depths of the ocean, where silliness flows,
Swim fish with top hats, and seaweed in prose.
The bubbles are giggles, released from the deep,
As we flounder and splash, forgetting to creep.

Glimmers of laughter drift softly around,
Echoes are whispers of joy they have found.
Sea turtles waltz while the crabs play their drums,
A chorus of chuckles from all of their homes.

Each wave holds a secret, a jest and a tale,
With dolphins of humor that happily sail.
Splashing and diving through jellyfish beams,
We find our reflection in whimsy and dreams.

So dive deep, my friend, and swim wild with delight,
In the echoes that shimmer, pure laughter takes flight.
A journey in currents of quirky and round,
Where joy's the horizon, and silliness bound.

Treasures of the Holding Hands

With fingers entwined, we embark on our quest,
In a world full of treasures, it's laughter that's best.
We frolic through fields, our feet light as air,
An adventure of giggles, with joy we will share.

Each grip a reminder of moments we've caught,
With jesters and jest, every tickle a thought.
A scavenger hunt for the quirkiest things,
We'll share our finds, like two clowns with bright rings.

As we wander together through paths lined with glee,
We stumble on secrets, like how to climb a tree.
From candy to daisies, each treasure we gain,
Brings bursts of laughter, a whimsical chain.

So here's to our holding, our hands clasped in cheer,
Collecting the moments that make our hearts clear.
With the wealth of our joy and the quirks that we sow,
We forge a bright legacy wherever we go.

Chains of Love's Legacy

In a drawer of memories, they hide,
Colorful links with a time-told pride.
Each charm a giggle, a tickle, a tease,
Jokes embedded in moments like these.

Like rubber bands stretched through the years,
Twisting and turning, igniting the cheers.
They squeak when they bounce, they dance with the light

Reminding us all that life's crown fits just right.

In a tangle of colors, our laughter remains,
With jingling stories like musical chains.
We wear 'em with chuckles, a grin that's contagious,
In each little trinket, the joy is outrageous.

So gather the links of your wildest dreams,
A bouquet of memories bursting at seams.
Each laugh like a charm, each smile a delight,
Chains of our love, forever in sight.

Threads of Boundless Wonder

Weaving together the fabric of fun,
Threads of our whims, oh, how they run!
Knots made of giggles, loops kissed by grace,
Patchworks of tales, let's dance in this space.

Stitching the moments with sunlight and glee,
Colors all mixed up – what will it be?
A quilt of adventures, stitched tight with cheer,
Life's a carnival, come spin it, my dear!

Pull on a thread, and watch it unwind,
It takes us to places, oh what will we find?
A tapestry woven from laughter and play,
Each stitch a reminder that joy's here to stay.

So let's spin our stories, each laughter a hue,
In a loom of delight, it's me and you.
Threads of adventure, never to sever,
In a patchwork of joy, we're light as a feather.

Spirals of Unwritten Stories

In spirals of paper, our tales intertwine,
Unwritten adventures, oh how they shine!
A twist of the pen, a swirl of delight,
Creating legacies that dance in the night.

Like spaghetti tossed with a fork of surprise,
Every loop a moment we must realize.
Some tales are silly, some gentle and sweet,
With each scribbled spiral, our heart skips a beat.

The stories unfold with a giggle and wiggle,
Chasing our dreams with a curious giggle.
Ink flows like water, our voices connect,
In spirals of laughter, there's nothing we regret.

So write down your whims, let your spirit take flight,
In a swirl of the fantastic, we dance through the night.
Spirals of journeys, forever evolving,
In pages of wonder, our lives are resolving.

Ornaments of the Heart's Journey

Hanging on branches, our hearts tell a tale,
Ornaments shining, in sunshine they sail.
Each flake of laughter, each glistening tear,
A reminder to treasure the moments so dear.

From hints of mischief to acts so sincere,
We deck out our days till the end of the year.
Baubles of joy, and tinsel of dreams,
Adventure awaits in the moonlight's soft beams.

With every little trinket comes laughter anew,
Collecting our stories like petals of dew.
In this wondrous garden, a glow we can share,
Ornaments linger, with stories laid bare.

So hang up your memories, twirl in delight,
With each little sparkle, we dance through the night.
Ornaments of laughter, forever we'll find,
In the journey of hearts, we're beautifully intertwined.

The Jewelry of Experience

In a land where socks do dance,
And pets recite a silly prance.
Each trinket holds a laugh or tear,
As stories weave, we shed no fear.

A locket filled with tales so bright,
Holds secrets shared in dark of night.
A bracelet made of candy wraps,
For good times had and endless laps.

Rings that jingle, hats that twirl,
In this realm, we laugh and whirl.
Gems of joy in laughter cast,
In dances spun, we hold them fast.

So gather round, let jokes be spun,
In this fine art, we've all had fun.
With each new piece, our hearts expand,
The jewelry of life, all hand in hand.

Threads of Love and Journey

In stitches bright, the memories grow,
From friendly chats to howling shows.
A scarf that warms when tales unfold,
And blankets thick with laughter bold.

With every knot, a giggle blooms,
In cozy nooks and bustling rooms.
A tapestry of friendship strong,
Each thread a note in laughter's song.

We wear our tales like badges proud,
Embroidered quirks that draw a crowd.
From soft embraces to trips afar,
The journey's joys shine like a star.

So spin the yarn, let life be bright,
With threads of love that ignite the night.
In every fiber, joy's refrain,
In every stitch, we dance again.

Interwoven Sentiments

In scraps of fabric, stories creep,
A patchwork quilt, a secret heap.
Each square a smile, each stitch a thread,
Holding warm laughter without dread.

A pocket watch that teases time,
Ticking tales with a silly rhyme.
In dancing stitches, memories flow,
As goofy antics steal the show.

With every fiber, we weave our fate,
From hugs so tight to jokes we state.
The fabric holds our joys and fears,
In playful antics, shedding tears.

So let us stitch our lives in cheer,
With interwoven thoughts sincere.
For laughter's fabric binds us tight,
In quirky threads, we find our light.

Bindings of the Heart's Chorus

In melodies of laughter wide,
Our hearts play tunes, side by side.
With jingles light, we sing our dreams,
As whimsical joy flows through our seams.

A chorus formed from silly notes,
In every giggle, magic floats.
With harmonies of friendship true,
Each binding brightens all we do.

So gather 'round, let voices rise,
Beneath the stars, we claim the skies.
In silly dances, our spirits soar,
With rhythmic laughter, we want more.

The heart's own song can never cease,
In bindings sweet, we find our peace.
With every note, we celebrate,
In laughter's arms, we seal our fate.

Interlaced Histories of the Heart

When love's a noodle, twirled with glee,
A plate of joy, just you and me.
All tangled up in laughter's tune,
Dancing 'neath the smiling moon.

Socks mismatched, yet hearts align,
Jokes shared over cheap red wine.
Each quirk a tale, a silly rhyme,
In our own space, we freeze the time.

The wobbly table's quite a show,
Like our love, it sways to and fro.
We scribble dreams on napkin scraps,
Embracing chaos, napping laps.

With every giggle, threads unite,
We weave our worlds, a comical sight.
In every flaw, we find delight,
In this crazy dance, our hearts take flight.

In the Weave of Existence

Life is a tapestry, bright and spry,
When colors clash, oh how they fly!
A sock with holes, a shirt that's bold,
In this wacky world, we dare to mold.

Quirky moments stitched with grace,
We wear our quirks like a playful lace.
Dancing on rainbows, slipping on ice,
Finding the joy in every slice.

Coffee cups tipped, laughter spills free,
We brew the chaos, wouldn't you agree?
A patchwork quilt, absurd but true,
We stitch our lives with a goofy hue.

In every twist, a comedic bend,
Life's a joke, but it's quite the blend.
With each odd yarn, our hearts expand,
In the weave of existence, hand in hand.

Chains of Thought and Emotion

Clanking thoughts like rusty chains,
They rattle on, a dance of brains.
Jokes and puns in tangled knots,
Our minds race wild, a circus lot.

We clip and clank, a giggling spree,
Thoughts collide with silly glee.
A mind's a mess, a lovely fray,
The heart joins in with a jazzy play.

In the scrapyard of our dreams,
Bizarre ideas burst at the seams.
Link by link, laughter unfurls,
Jingling with fun, our joy just swirls.

Connecting dots with a wink and nod,
In this chain game, we strut and trod.
Thoughts and feelings, an amusing blend,
In our quirky saga, let the laughter lend.

Threads of Fate and Free Will

Fate hands out threads, bright and frayed,
We make our clothes, unafraid.
With every stitch, we laugh and twirl,
Twisting tales in a whirly whirl.

Where destiny trips, humor wakes,
We'll strum our paths with silly shakes.
A chance encounter, a pie in the face,
In the fabric of life, it's all a race.

Free will dances on a soapbox high,
While fate cracks jokes that make us sigh.
Pulling the strings with laughter's might,
In this wavy world, we'll take flight.

Threads intertwine, a patchwork spree,
Creating a quilt of sheer jubilee.
In fate we trust, but let's be clear,
Life's a party—let's get a cheer!

Symbols of the Ethereal Bond

In a land where rubber reigns,
The boldest styles, they wear no chains.
Twisted colors, shades of glee,
Dance on wrists, so carefree!

Some say it's just a gimmick flair,
But look closer, if you dare.
Each hue a tale, each twist a joke,
Binding folks like a jovial cloak!

Friends in mismatched pairs, we strut,
One orange, one green, oh what a cut!
Laughter echoes, as we parade,
Our silly bonds, never to fade!

In the end, all's in good fun,
These colorful bands, a bond begun.
So wear them tight, or let them slide,
In our hearts, forever tied!

Chords of the Heart's Echo

Strumming beats on tender arms,
Colors clash, spreading charms.
Each one jingles with delight,
As we skip through day and night.

Some might call it silly flair,
But what's life without some dare?
With twirls and jumps, we peel away,
The mundane rules of every day!

A blue one speaks of pizza nights,
While the yellow shouts of playful fights.
In laughter, bonds are tightly spun,
Chords resonate, we're never done!

A rainbow chorus, we unite,
In our playful, quirky plight.
No dullness here, just vibrant cheer,
Each heartbeat sings, our love sincere!

Whispers in Colorful Threads

Woven tales in colors bright,
Whispers giggle, taking flight.
Loop and knot, a playful cheer,
Feel the magic, hold it near.

There's a red one for your lunch surprise,
And a pink that knows how to rise!
They twirl and twist, a silly dance,
Caught in friendship's playful trance.

Threads of laughter, not just thread,
Stories linger, though they spread.
In every color, joy is spun,
Together we laugh, together we run!

So let's adorn our wrists with flair,
Mix and match without a care.
Let worries float, let spirits gleam,
In playful threads, we live our dream!

Entwined in Spirit

Tangled lines in colors bold,
Bonds that shimmer, never cold.
Wristy wonders, all around,
Fueling joy where love is found.

With every twist, a new embrace,
Friends together, we find our place.
Banshee bands with stories shared,
In bright designs, our hearts laid bare!

A whimsical twist to every tale,
Colors swirl, we never fail.
Zany patterns make us grin,
In this dance, we always win!

So clasp your friends, don't let go,
In this laughter, let's all grow.
Bound by joy, through thick and thin,
With playful threads, we always win!

Woven Stories of Existence

In a world of silly strings,
We dance with joyful flings.
Each color tells a tale,
Of mishaps, laughs, and ale.

Twisted knots that never quit,
Catch my shoe and make me split.
From blue to green, a vibrant mess,
Life's a game, we must confess.

Elastic dreams around our arms,
Hold our laughs, our quirky charms.
An orange hue, a yellow grin,
Look at all this fun we're in!

So gather 'round, let's tie them tight,
In this crazy, carefree night.
With every loop, our spirits soar,
Woven tales forevermore.

Accents of the Whispering Soul

A sage once wore a ribbon bright,
Said it spoke of day and night.
But truth be told, it's just a game,
Now everyone thinks I'm quite lame.

My friend adorned in polka dots,
Says it shows her thinky thoughts.
But all I hear is squeaky fun,
When she trips and starts to run.

Pinks and purples, wild and free,
Life's a riddle, can't you see?
We whisper dreams of giggles near,
As sanity takes flight, oh dear!

So let's compare our fancy threads,
In a world that often spreads.
For in the end, it's clear to see,
These accents make us, you and me.

Links of Radiant Laughter

Oh, the colors that we wear,
Bring a smile everywhere.
Each link a twist, a jest, a cheer,
With every pull, we shed a tear.

I tied a chain of jiggly beads,
Grew a garden full of seeds.
Some sprouted giggles on the way,
Who knew they'd bloom in such a sway?

Doodles drawn on plastic bands,
Tell our dreams and clever plans.
Ink that spills just like my thoughts,
Becoming patterns, tangled knots.

So here's a toast to wobbly fun,
To every joke that's just begun.
With every laugh, let's dance and sing,
Our radiant links make life a fling!

Adorning the Invisible Tapestry

Life's a quilt of crazy threads,
Stitched with laughter, worn like spreads.
A patch of giggles, a dash of cheers,
Adorning all our laughter years.

With every color, there's a tale,
Of silly slips and epic fails.
Like a ride on a rollercoaster,
Tossed around a joyful poster.

The invisible patterns we wear,
Hold memories of silly flair.
From mischief done with flair and grace,
These woven laughs we can't erase.

So grab your thread, let's weave anew,
In this tapestry, me and you.
For with each stitch, our tales unfold,
A funny life, a bond of gold.

Threads of the Heart's Embrace

In the closet of emotions, colors spin,
Like a clown in a circus, where all things begin.
Stripes of laughter, polka dots of cheer,
Twist and turn, like we have no fear.

Haphazard stitches that fray and bloom,
Dancing around like a wild vacuum.
Bright neon threads weave tales of delight,
In the loom of our heart, everything feels right.

Laughter's the glue, though sticky and bold,
We wear it like magic, a wondrous fold.
Tangled together, a ridiculous sight,
Yet in this chaos, our spirits take flight.

So let's stitch a story, with zany designs,
Woven together, our fate intertwines.
With fabric so vibrant, absurd and bright,
We embrace the chaos, and it feels just right.

Echoes in the Fabric of Being

In the threads of our tales, a giggle resounds,
Echoes of joy where silliness abounds.
Fabrics unwrapping like jokes in the air,
Crafted by life, and we wear them with flair.

Twirling and swirling, the ribbons do play,
Each twist tells a joke, in a quirky way.
The seams may unravel, but that's part of the game,
For laughter and joy are the threads that we claim.

Beneath all the layers, the shenanigans flow,
Snippets of nonsense in patterns that glow.
A patchwork of moments, both funny and bright,
Stitched with the quirks that amuse our own sight.

So let's dance through the fabric, in stitches so bold,
Thread our tomfoolery, let the fun unfold.
In the quilt of our being, may hilarity reign,
For a life sewn with laughter is never in vain.

Ties that Bind the Inner Light

In the knots of our souls, giggles are tied,
Like shoelaces tangled, we wear with pride.
Cotton candy dreams and unruly threads,
We stumble through laughter, safe in our beds.

A spool of mischief rolls under the chair,
While jokes tie us closer, without a care.
Witty barbs woven from whimsy and cheer,
The fabric of friendship is what we hold dear.

Tangled together in a whimsical dance,
Where each trip and fall is a daring chance.
The strings may be frayed, but that's how we shine,
In the mess of our laughter, our hearts intertwine.

So gather your colors, let the fun play,
Embrace every stitch of this glorious fray.
For the ties that connect us are silly and bright,
Bringing smiles in the dark, an incandescent light.

Adornments of the Spirit's Journey

In the carnival of life, we wear our flair,
With gaudy charms dazzling everywhere.
Each trinket a story, each bead a jest,
In the wind of our laughter, we feel so blessed.

Spangles and sparkles, oh what a show,
Twirling in chaos, we giggle and glow.
Adornments of joy, with a pinch of the wild,
We embrace our weirdness, each spirit a child.

A tapestry woven with whimsy and fun,
A parade of oddities, we run and we run.
In the grand bazaar of what makes us whole,
Every laugh is a jewel that shines in the soul.

So deck yourself out, let your colors combine,
For in this mad journey, the joy is divine.
With adornments so silly, we'll dance through the night,
On this wild, strange path, everything feels right.

Bands of Connection Beyond Time

In a world of rubber and flair,
We wear our memories with care.
A green one for pizza nights,
And red for the epic fights!

Each color tells a silly tale,
Of mishaps that never grow stale.
The blue one dances like it's free,
While the yellow one just spills my tea!

They stretch and bend with every laugh,
These bands keep track of my gaffe.
A bracelet's bond that won't unwind,
As silly thoughts we hope to find!

So here's to bands that stretch so wide,
They capture joy, our hearts confide.
In every hue, a moment glows,
With silly secrets only we know!

The Colors of Inner Harmony

I wore a purple for my mood,
While the orange made me feel so crude.
A rainbow wraps my wrist with cheer,
As laughter dances, drawing near.

The teal reminds me of my cat,
While the pink screams, "Hey, how about that?"
Each shade reflects my daily grind,
In hues of madness, joy entwined!

The gold says I'm rich in fun,
But also might weigh a ton!
With every flick of my wrist,
I juggle colors, can't resist!

Let's raise a toast with wristbands bright,
To all our quirks that feel so right.
In this silly color spree,
Who knew my stress could wear a glee?

Emblems of One's Essence

These trinkets swirl with charm and grace,
As goofball memories we embrace.
A dinosaur for my late-night snack,
And stripes to keep the goofy knack!

Each emblem holds its own sweet tale,
From epic fails to dancing snail.
The silver sparkles like my gaze,
While the polka dots sing quirky praise!

My treasures twirl in playful glee,
With whispers of who I choose to be.
A wrist adorned with colors bright,
Each emblem gleaming in daylight!

So let us wear this silly pride,
With badges of nonsense as our guide.
A laugh, a smile, a memory,
In these trinkets, I find pure glee!

Symbols Woven in Silence

In the quiet of the evening glow,
My wristbands chat, they start to flow.
The ones that slice like cheddar cheese,
And wink at life with silly tease!

Each twist and turn a silent shout,
As colors dance and flail about.
The purple whispers jokes unspoken,
While the green one claims it's never broken!

They tickle my thoughts, each strand a grin,
With every tug, a chance to spin.
In silence, stories gently brew,
While the rubber bands form a crazy crew!

So here we gather, quirky friends,
With laughter that never ends.
In the silence, we find our song,
With bands that help us get along!

The Fabric of Our Belonging

In a world of thread and twine,
We're stitched together, looking fine.
With patterns odd and colors bright,
We laugh and dance, a silly sight.

Each loop and knot, a tale to tell,
Of moments shared, how we fell.
With crafty hands, we weave our fate,
In this fabric, there's no debate.

A patchwork quilt of joy and cheer,
Stuck together, year by year.
We flaunt our styles, we wear them proud,
Like walking art, we draw a crowd.

So let's embrace this craziness,
In every fray, we find our bliss.
For in this weave of laughs and dreams,
We're tied together, or so it seems.

Light Caught in a Ribbonscape

Twirling ribbons in the sun,
Chasing shadows, just for fun.
With every tug and playful spin,
We collect the joy that lies within.

A rainbow burst, we wave around,
In this ribbonscape, laughter's found.
With every twist, and playful snap,
We tie our hearts in a goofy clap.

Glimmers dance like fireflies,
In our silly tricks, the light defies.
We're a circus of giggles, gleeful strikes,
Crafting memories, like bike rides and hikes.

So let's weave magic in the air,
Through tangled threads, beyond compare.
As light caught in ribbons takes its flight,
We find our joy in sheer delight.

Shadows Transformed into Luminescence

When shadows play, they tell a joke,
They twist and turn, like a feathered cloak.
With every whisper of the night,
We giggle softly, chasing light.

In the dark, goofballs do appear,
Casting shapes that dance with cheer.
A shadow puppet circus bright,
Fills the world with pure delight.

From gloom to glow, we skip along,
With lively beats and silly song.
We laugh at what the darkness brings,
Transforming it into joyful flings.

So embrace the night, let shadows play,
In the luminescence we find our way.
For even in dark, we have the knack,
To shine our laughter, never lack.

Colors that Speak without Words

In every hue, a laughter stirs,
A splash of fun, where joy occurs.
Each shade a giggle, bright and loud,
A palette made for the silliest crowd.

With crayons drawn, we doodle dreams,
In quirky lines, our laughter beams.
A masterpiece of whimsy flows,
In every stroke, our humor glows.

From reds so bold to blues so deep,
Colors chat while laughter leaps.
In giggling shades that never tire,
We paint our world with pure desire.

So let's embrace this vibrant show,
Where colors sing and giggles grow.
We speak in shades, loud and clear,
In this carnival of joy, my dear.

Bracelets of Memory and Hope

In vibrant colors they twirl with glee,
A reminder of laughter, just like a spree.
Each twist and turn, a story we spin,
Who knew a simple band could start such a din?

They jingle and jangle, a cheerful crew,
With secrets to share, and good vibes too.
When life gets sticky, we choose to wear,
These charms of delight, with a carefree flair!

Caught in the fun, we dance through the day,
With memories bright, like a child at play.
Together we forge this whimsical chain,
Woven with friendship, it banishes pain!

So slip on a band, let your worries be,
For life's too short, let's giggle with glee.
We'll toast to the moments that make us feel whole,
With these little trinkets, we'll shine like a coal!

Emblems of the Unseen Journey

Through thick and thin, we march side by side,
These quirky emblems, our joy, our pride.
From zany colors to shapes quite absurd,
Each one's a badge for the craziest herd!

They jostle and jive, in rhythmic display,
With tales untold that are just a short play.
Adventurers dressed in our finest array,
Each mile we travel, we laugh all the way!

Like breadcrumbs of portals to where we have been,
Through chuckles and stumbles, we wear our best grin.
These odd little bands will keep us in line,
As we frolic through life, sipping punch from a vine!

When grumpy clouds gather, we look to our loot,
With colors so bright, how can we dispute?
Let's dance under them, we know how to cope,
As we chime in together, with humor and hope!

Bands of Resonant Dreams

Worn on the wrist, like a pop star's fling,
Each band a secret, an unspoken thing.
With laughter and whimsy, we bounce and we hop,
Collecting our dreams, we'll never, not stop!

In wacky designs, they gleefully clash,
Our visions of future, in a colorful flash.
They shimmer and sparkle, they wriggle and wave,
Silly reminders that we are quite brave!

From daytime delights to night-time's embrace,
Our bands hold the charm of our wildest chase.
When faced with a challenge, we chuckle and cheer,
For with these bright trinkets, our path is so clear!

So wear them with pride, let your spirit run free,
These bands of our dreams hold the essence of me.
With each jolly jingle, our folly is told,
In the dance of our hearts, we are never too old!

Links of Silent Understanding

In vibrant hues, we find our own tune,
These links so quirky, they make laughter swoon.
With giggles and nods, we join hand in hand,
In this game of life, what a wacky band!

When words fail us, we smile and we grin,
These links are our language; it's where we begin.
With winks and a nudge, we bond with great flair,
No words are needed, just a soul laid bare!

Through thick and thin, they clink with delight,
A chuckle or two under moonlit night.
With tales in our hearts and jest in our veins,
We share in the joy, and it never wanes!

So here's to the links that connect us all,
We'll tumble through life, we'll laugh and we'll call.
In silly camaraderie, our spirits align,
With these whimsical links, together we shine!

Mementos of Celestial Embrace

In a world where rubber meets the day,
Colors dance and laugh, come what may.
Twirled around wrists, they giggle and sing,
Whispers of joy in this playful bling.

Bouncing with secrets, each color a joke,
Fluorescent friendships that glitter and poke.
A pink one for laughter, a green one for fun,
Together they shine like the bright midday sun.

When they get tangled, a messy delight,
Fingers entwined in a colorful fight.
"Who wore it worse?" becomes the new game,
As foes become friends in this wild, silly fame.

In every squish and every twist,
Is a sprinkle of humor that can't be missed.
Each charm tells a story, each band takes a turn,
In laughter so loud, our spirits do burn.

Adorned Hearts in Harmony

With bands of bright hues, we gather in glee,
Decorated joyfully, just you and me.
Every bangle's a tune, a rhythm, a step,
In our dance of delight, there's no need for prep.

Peeking out from under our sleeves,
The secrets they hold, nobody believes!
A tale of mishaps, an epic or two,
Every twist and turn makes our laughter renew.

What's red for embarrassment? What's blue for despair?
In this colorful chaos, we lay our hearts bare.
Like jellybeans popping, we chuckle and grin,
Life's a sweet journey, a whimsical spin.

Come sit in this circus, let's share all our charms,
With laughter that weaves us, safe in its arms.
From pinkies to thumbs, we'll link up our fate,
In this wild party of joy, let's celebrate!

The Fabric of Unspoken Truth

Threads of bright colors, they mumble and cheer,
Bringing together the laughs, the dear.
In a twirl of fabric, confusion takes flight,
As friendships turn nonsense into pure delight.

One band for your coffee, one for your snack,
Wrapped around stories that never hold back.
Each elastic's a chapter, a giggle or howl,
In this cloth of connection, we all take a bow.

A tangled design that tickles the heart,
Stretching our humor, that silly old art.
Through the twists and turns, we find our own truth,
Each laugh a reminder of our timeless youth.

So let's wear our stripes, let's flaunt our bright hues,
In this carnival of life, we'll never lose.
With smiles and shadows, let's dance to the tune,
In the fabric of laughter, beneath the same moon.

Unity in Delicate Strands

Oh look at the strands, they're jiggling right there,
A rainbow of giggles fluffs up in the air.
From stretch to snap, they shimmy and glide,
Holding our stories and a whole lot of pride.

Each twist and each twirl brings a laugh to the fray,
In this wristy adventure, we'll jostle and play.
With sparkles that chatter, and patterns so bright,
Our souls interwoven, a whimsical sight.

What's orange for mischief? What's yellow for cheer?
In this joyful exchange, we have nothing to fear.
Together we stumble, but we never fall flat,
In a world full of laughter, we simply go splat!

So grab all your buddies, let's fill up our arms,
With strands of connection and playful charms.
In the circus of life, we're the jesters, it's true,
With colors of joy that always shine through.

Ties that Bind the Spirit

In the land where socks go to hide,
Mismatched souls run wild with pride.
A rubber band stretched, oh what a sight,
Looped and tangled, ready for flight.

We dance in circles, no need to cry,
With silly hats, we reach for the sky.
Each giggle wraps tight, a shimmering thread,
Binding us closer, no need for dread.

Like friendship bracelets, tossed in the fray,
Twisted and knotted, we find our way.
With laughter as glue, we stick like glue,
Our ties are the quirks that make us true.

So come on and join, don't let it slide,
With each silly step, let's joyfully glide.
For in this mess, we find our role,
The ties we create, they bind the soul!

Remnants of Heartstrings

On the fridge, memories dangle and sway,
Like old pizza boxes from yesterday.
Each love note scribbled in crayon bright,
A symphony of laughter, pure delight.

With a wink and a nudge, we poke fun at fate,
As we twirl in a dance, it's never too late.
A mishmash of yarn, spun from our dreams,
We're crafting a quilt of giggles and schemes.

Hearts stitched together with thread that's unbroken,
In every punchline, words left unspoken.
Each tickle of joy, a sweet serenade,
Echoing softly, in laughter we're made.

So let's toss our socks, those mismatched affairs,
For life is a canvas, we paint with glares.
In the remnants of love, we'll find our scores,
Strings of hilarity, forever outdoors!

Adornments of the Inner Flame

In a world where marshmallows reign supreme,
We wear silly hats, our whimsical theme.
With cupcakes galore and sprinkles on top,
Our inner flame dances, it never will stop.

Like spaghetti noodles tossed in the air,
We twirl our quirks, without a care.
Each laugh a bead on our dazzling string,
Our joy is the bling that we all shall bring.

So grab your kazoo, let's make some noise,
The butterflies flutter, oh what a choice!
In this carnival of hearts, we all ignite,
With merriment twinkling, our spirits take flight.

Come gather 'round, let's create some glee,
With a wink and a wink, just you wait and see.
We wear our laughter, it shines like a flame,
Adornments of joy, we'll never be tame!

Tokens of Eternal Whispers

In the attic of dreams where doodles collide,
We find tiny treasures that we cannot hide.
Like paper airplanes that soar in the breeze,
Whispers of laughter that bring us to knees.

With giggles exchanged like rare golden coins,
We barter our stories as joy never joins.
Each secret a token, so sweet and absurd,
In the game of our lives, we're totally stirred.

So let's wear our quirks like a badge of delight,
With each friendly poke, we'll light up the night.
For in every chuckle, life's magic unfolds,
Eternal whispers, more precious than gold.

So treasure these moments, both silly and bright,
With hearts stitched together, we'll dance through the night.
For in this wild journey, we've found our bliss,
These tokens we cherish, we'll never dismiss!

Talismans of Shared Experience

We wear our joy like funky charms,
A band of laughter that disarms.
Each twist and turn, a memory spun,
Together we laugh, together we run.

In mismatched hues and silly styles,
Our bands tell tales with goofy smiles.
From secret codes to dance-off bets,
These vibrant ties, we won't forget.

Each hug a knot, each dance a thread,
With every heartbeat, mischief is spread.
So let's create a tapestry bright,
Of friendship woven through day and night.

With every slip, a secret kept,
In rubber threads, our laughter leapt.
So here's to bonds that bend and twist,
In our silly world, we coexist.

Echoes Upon the Wrist

Echoes bounce like rubber bands,
Vibrating tales across the stands.
A flick of wrist, a laugh or two,
Our history wraps us like glue.

A splash of color, a dash of flair,
We trade our tales without a care.
Chronicles whispered with every glance,
In playful steps, we join the dance.

Each color speaks of moments bright,
Of pizza nights and silly fights.
From clumsy falls to epic fails,
Our wrist-bound tales send joyful mails.

In knots of fortune, we're entwined,
Tickled by fortune, laughter defined.
So let's embrace our quirky quest,
In every twist, we find the best.

Encircled by Emotion's Dance

Around our wrists, emotions sway,
A disco beat that leads the way.
In every twirl, a giggle sneaks,
Our pulse a rhythm, laughter peaks.

Bright bands that sing our hearts' refrain,
From silly jokes to friendly pain.
Encircled tight, but never wound,
In joyful chaos, love is found.

Each color glows with stories shared,
In clapping hands, how much we dared.
With silly pranks and wild designs,
Our tangles thrive on happy signs.

So dance with me in this parade,
Where every bond is brightly displayed.
With every heartbeat, we advance,
In our strange worlds, we take a chance.

Pulse of Past Affections

The pulse of joy, it bounces bright,
A band of laughter in morning light.
Each twang a tale, a vintage whine,
Of crazed adventures, yours and mine.

With each elastic stretch we sway,
Reminded of those wacky days.
Our laughter wraps around our hands,
In silly tricks, true life expands.

A rainbow of mishaps and dreams,
Together bursting at the seams.
In every twist, we find a spark,
Lighting up our silly arc.

So raise a toast with every snap,
In the fabric of laughter, take a nap.
For in the pulse of joys we've worn,
A world of wonders still is born.

Charms of the Forgotten Path

In the garden of lost socks, they play,
Dancing lightly, brightening the gray.
With mismatched shoes and a wink so sly,
They whisper secrets as the day goes by.

A paisley scarf, it tells a tale,
Of nights under stars and an old ship's sail.
It trips on laughter, clumsily blooms,
A jester perched high, casting away glooms.

Beneath the porch, a button rides,
With edges smooth and tales that guide.
It helps the sun in a friendly race,
Turning tears into smiles—oh, what a place!

So join the parade, don't miss the bus,
With hats so big, we raise a fuss.
For in the charm, we find the jest,
Life's a carnival, simply the best!

Clasping the Infinite

In the realm where oddities thrive,
A rubber band's laugh can surely dive.
It bounces back with a jolly grin,
Slinging joy like a mischievous twin.

A shoelace long, with stories to tell,
It ties the universe, oh so well.
When knots are made, they dance and twirl,
Creating a mess—what a wild swirl!

An old keyring holds the dreams we've lost,
Each buckle and twist is a tale embossed.
They jingle and jangle to the beat of cheer,
Reminding us all that fun's always near.

So clasp your joys with a grin so wide,
Let laughter echo, come along for the ride.
For in this quirky, infinite span,
Life's a comedy, oh yes, it can!

Ribbons of Inner Light

A tangle of ribbons in colors so bright,
Each twist and turn, a spark of delight.
They giggle and flutter upon the breeze,
Painting the skies with giggles and ease.

The knots hold secrets of spirits so bold,
Stories of laughter that never grow old.
They skip and hop with a playful shout,
In the carnival of dreams, they twirl about.

In pockets of happiness, they find their place,
Unraveling mysteries with each embrace.
A bright yellow strand whispers, 'Life's a blast!'
While purple giggles, 'Let's have some fun fast!'

So twirl in the ribbons, let chaos ignite,
Dance to the rhythm of pure delight.
In this tapestry woven with Heart's embrace,
Every laughter echo, a timeless grace!

Artifacts of the Spirit's Voyage

A compass spins, lost in its dreams,
Chasing the laughter more than it seems.
With directions that vanish, it winks at fate,
Sending us off to a whimsical state.

The treasure map's scribbles make little sense,
Leading us to where joy is immense.
Each X on the plot marks a gag surprise,
So pack up your chuckles and open your eyes!

An hourglass pours giggles instead of sand,
Tickling the moments we once had planned.
It tells us no hurry, just let it flow,
In joy's gentle stream, where laughter will grow.

So gather these artifacts, join the fun spree,
In the voyage of souls, there's so much to see.
Let whimsy be your guide, take a grand leap,
For in the humor of life, our hearts take a leap!

www.ingramcontent.com/pod-product-compliance
Lightning Source LLC
Chambersburg PA
CBHW060124230426
43661CB00003B/320